Devon Gets the Common Cold

By Carmel Reilly

Devon and Dad went to the park.

"This blossom smells great,"
said Dad.

"I can not smell it," said Devon.

At home, Devon said,
"Dad, I feel ill."

"Get into bed," said Dad.
"I will bring you a sweet
lemon drink."

"Should I go to the doctor?"
said Devon.

"No," said Dad. "It's just
a common cold."

"Do I need to stay in bed with just a common cold?" said Devon. "I will be so bored!"

"You need to rest," said Dad.
"And you must protect other
people from getting it from you."

Dad got Devon some books.

"Shall I read this one to you?"
he said.

"Yes, please," said Devon.

Soon, she was sleeping.

The next day, Devon still felt sick.

Dad got her a second sweet lemon drink.

Devon picked up a book.

She was reading her second book when Dad came in with carrot and bacon soup.

Dad got Devon some wool,
buttons and ribbons.

"I can make a toy lion with this
today!" said Devon.

By the end of the day,
Devon did not feel sick.

"You can get up tomorrow,"
said Dad.

"But I like being in bed!"
said Devon.

Dad sneezed.

Then he sneezed a second time!

"Now I have a cold!" he said.

You are lucky, Dad.
I had a good lesson in helping
a person with a common cold!

CHECKING FOR MEANING

1. What did Devon do when Dad was reading to her? *(Literal)*

2. What did Devon use to make the toy lion? *(Literal)*

3. Why couldn't Devon smell the blossom at the park? *(Inferential)*

EXTENDING VOCABULARY

blossom	What is a *blossom*? What trees do you know that have blossoms? What is another word that has a similar meaning to *blossom*?
common	What is the meaning of *common* in this story? Why is Devon's illness called a *common cold*?
protect	What do you do if you *protect* someone or something? What things do you protect? Who helps to protect you?

MOVING BEYOND THE TEXT

1. Talk about why bees can often be seen on blossoms. What are they looking for? Why?

2. Discuss the symptoms of the common cold, such as a blocked nose, sore throat and a cough. Talk about how this makes you feel.

3. Ask students to explain how they can prevent germs spreading to other people, e.g. cover your nose and mouth when you cough, wash your hands often, stay away from other people.

4. Retell a time when you were unwell and someone had to take care of you. What illness did you have? Who cared for you? How did they help you to get better?

THE SCHWA

| a | e | i | o | u |

PRACTICE WORDS

the

protect

blossom

Devon

carrot

lemon

second

bacon

ribbons

lesson

buttons

lion

a

common

person

The